An npower publication
First published in Great Britain in 2007 by Npower Limited
Oak House, 1 Bridgwater Road, Warndon, Worcester, Worcestershire WR4 9FP
www.npower.com

© Npower Limited 2007

All rights reserved. No part of this publication may be reproduced, stored in a retrieval system, or transmitted in any form or by any means, electronic, mechanical, photocopying, recording or otherwise, without the prior permission of the copyright holder.

ISBN 978-0-9555349-0-4

The publishers and authors have made every effort to ensure the accuracy and currency of the information in The npower Book of Light. The publisher and authors disclaim any liability, loss, injury or damage incurred as a consequence, directly or indirectly, of the use and application of the contents of this book.

Book of Light

The nation's top 100 light bulb jokes
as judged by Lenny Henry

Foreword

Bright spark, Thomas Edison, lit up the first ever light bulb in 1879. Since that time, light bulb jokes have gradually become a national institution – like the Beatles, Marmite or a nice cup of tea.

npower Book of Light

To celebrate these much loved riddles, and to raise awareness of energy saving in a light-hearted way, I have proudly joined forces with npower to find the best this country has to offer. Switched-on wannabe comedians, and those that appreciate a good giggle, have all submitted their favourite light bulb jokes to help us compile this definitive collection of the top 100.

The genius of the light bulb joke lies in its simplicity and adaptability. You can make a light bulb joke about pretty much anyone or anything and we encouraged the public to let their imaginations run riot. Selecting the top 100 involved a lot of healthy debate, as well as laughs, and the final collection includes everything from WAGs, to James Bond, to Take That, as well as some old classics.

A donation of £2 from **The npower Book of Light** will go to **Comic Relief** for **Red Nose Day 2007.** You can have a laugh and feel good about the fact that you have helped put a **big** smile on the face of someone who really needs it.

Lenny Henry

npower — Book of Light

1

Q. How many divorced men does it take to change a light bulb?
A. None: they never get the house.

npower   Book of Light

2
Q. How many Vietnam vets does it take to change a light bulb?
A. You don't know man, you weren't there!

3
Q. How many reality TV stars does it take to change a light bulb?
A. None: their time in the spotlight is over.

4

Q. How many real men does it take to change a light bulb?

A. None: real men aren't afraid of the dark.

npower   **Book of Light**

Q. One!
A. How many psychics does it take to change a light bulb?

5

6

Q. How many James Bond fans does it take to change a light bulb?
A. One to change it, and ten to complain that the original was better!

npower — Book of Light

7

Q. How many sex therapists does it take to change a light bulb?

A. Two: one to screw it in and one to tell him he's screwing it in the wrong way!

8 Q. How many roadies does it take to change a light bulb?
A. One, one-two, one-two...

9 Q. How many lawyers does it take to change a light bulb?
A. How many can you afford?

10

Q. How many women with PMT does it take to replace a light bulb?

A. One, because it just bloody does, all right!

11

Q. How many crime writers does it take to change a light bulb?
A. One, but there will have to be a real twist at the end.

12

Q. How many art museum visitors does it take to screw in a light bulb?
A. Two: one to do it and one to say, "My four-year-old could do that."

13

Q. How many poets does it take to change a light bulb?

A. One, but only if you can find a word to rhyme with light bulb...

npower | Book of Light

14
Q. How many anglers does it take to change a light bulb?
A. Five, and you should've seen the light bulb! It must have been ...*this*... big! (Gestures with arms...) Five of us were barely enough!

15
Q. How many Mafia Men does it take to change a light bulb?
A. Two: one to change the bulb and the other to shoot any witnesses!

16

Q. How many politicians does it take to change a light bulb?

A. Two: one to change it, and one to change it back again.

npower   **Book of Light**

17 **Q. How many fatalists does it take to screw in a light bulb?
A. It doesn't matter; we're all going to die anyway!**

18 **Q. How many surrealists does it take to change a light bulb?
A. Two: one to hold the giraffe, and the other to fill the bathtub with brightly-coloured machine tools.**

19

Q. How many optimists does it take to screw in a light bulb?
A. None: they're convinced that the power will come back on soon.

npower Book of Light

Q. How many drummers does it take to change a light bulb?
A. One... two and a one... two... three... four.

20

21

Q. How many magicians does it take to change a light bulb?

A. Depends on what you want to change it into.

Q. How many holy women does it take to change a light bulb?
A. Nun.

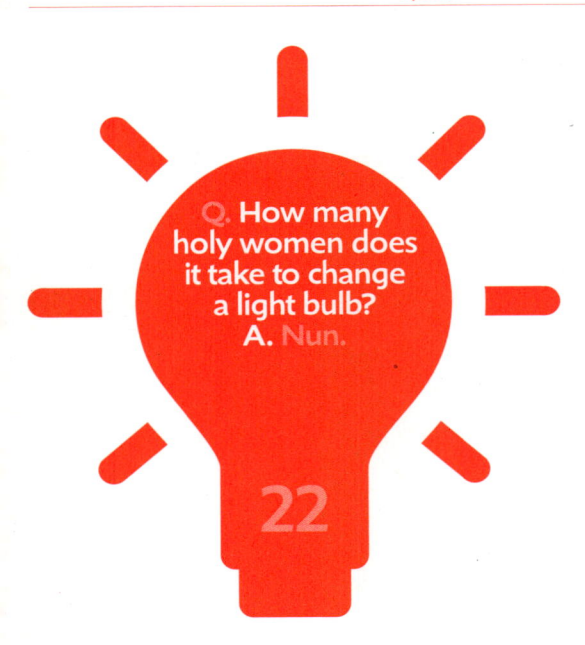

22

23

Q. How many economists does it take to screw in a light bulb?
A. None: if the light bulb really needed changing, market forces would have already caused it to happen.

npower — Book of Light

24

Q. How many philosophers does it take to change a light bulb?

A. Three: one to change it and two to stand around arguing over whether or not the light bulb exists.

npower — Book of Light

25
Q. How many perfectionists does it take to change a light bulb?
A. None: they changed it before it broke.

26
Q. **How many electricians does it take to change a light bulb?**
A. One: they're quite good at that sort of thing.

27

Q. How many hippies does it take to change a light bulb?

A. None: they respect it for what it is and wouldn't dream of trying to change it.

npower   Book of Light

28 **Q. How many yuppie women does it take to change a light bulb?
A. Two: one to mix the G&Ts and one to call the electrician.**

29 **Q. How many board meetings does it take to get a light bulb changed?
A. This topic was resumed from last week's discussion, but is incomplete pending resolution of some action items. It will be continued next week. Meanwhile...**

npower — Book of Light

30

Q. How many football managers does it take to change a light bulb?

A. Who knows, they're never around long enough to find out!

npower — Book of Light

31 Q. How many architects does it take to screw in a light bulb?
A. None: they can't get planning permission for the new one.

32 Q. How many amoebas does it take to change a light bulb?
A. 1, no ...2 ...4, no 8, 16 (etc, etc).

33

Q. How many wrestlers does it take to change a light bulb?

A. None: they don't want to be known as lightweights!

34 **Q. How many computer programmers does it take to screw in a light bulb?**
A. 011100110010...

35 **Q. How many freemasons does it take to change a light bulb?**
A. ...It's a secret.

36

Q. How many Man Utd players does it take to change a light bulb?

A. All eleven, as they are trying to persuade the referee that it doesn't need changing.

npower — Book of Light

37
Q. How many stand-up comedians does it take to change a light bulb?
A. Two: one to screw in the bulb and the other to say "Sock it to me!"

38
Q. How many members of Take That does it take to change a light bulb?
A. Four, but they'll have to give each other a leg-up as Robbie's stolen the ladder.

39

Q. How many flies does it take to screw in a light bulb?

A. Only two, but I don't know how they got in there.

npower — Book of Light

40 **Q. How many typical teenagers does it take to change a light bulb?
A. Who cares, it'll only blow again!**

41 **Q. How many facilities staff does it take to change a light bulb?
A. Five: one to carry the new light bulb, one to fill out the Health & Safety form, one to check that the one filling out the form doesn't hurt himself, a first aider, and another (least qualified to actually do the job).**

npower — Book of Light

42

Q. How many stockbrokers does it take to change a light bulb?

A. Two: one to take out the bulb and drop it, and the other to try and sell it before it crashes (knowing that it's already burned out).

npower · Book of Light

43 Q. **How many DIY buffs does it take to change a light bulb?**
A. Only one, but it takes him two weekends and three trips to the DIY store.

44 Q. How many scientists does it take to change a light bulb?
A. None: they all rely on the light of the future.

45

Q. How many maths students does it take to change a light bulb?

A. Twenty: one to change it, and the rest to watch and discuss how exciting it is.

46 **Q.** How many existentialists does it take to screw in a light bulb?
A. Two: one to screw it in, and one to observe how the light bulb itself symbolises a single incandescent beacon of subjective reality in a netherworld of endless absurdity reaching out toward a maudlin cosmos of nothingness.

47 **Q.** How many blondes does it take to screw in a light bulb?
A. 150: 1 to hold the bulb and 149 to turn the house!

npower | Book of Light

48

Q. How many divorce lawyers does it take to change a light bulb?

A. Three: one to argue for the rights of the old light bulb, one to argue for the rights of the new light bulb, and one to argue for the rights of the light socket.

49 Q. How many voyeurs does it take to change a light bulb?
A. Only one, but they'd much rather watch someone else do it!

50 Q. How many nuclear engineers does it take to change a light bulb?
A. Seven: one to install the new bulb and six to figure out what to do with the old one for the next 10,000 years.

51

Q. How many London cabbies does it take to change a light bulb?

A. Go all the way up there and come back empty? You must be kidding, mate.

npower   Book of Light

Q. How many divorced women does it take to change a light bulb?
A. Four: one to change the bulb and three to form a support group.

52

53

Q. How many Blue Peter presenters does it take to change a light bulb?
A. Two: one to change it, and one to turn the old one into an attractive Christmas tree decoration.

54

Q. How many folk singers does it take to change a light bulb?

A. Four: one to change the bulb and the other three to sing about how good the old one was!

55
Q. How many lawyers does it take to change a light bulb?
A. None: they all prefer to leave their clients in the dark.

56
Q. How many jugglers does it take to change a light bulb?
A. Only one, but it takes at least three light bulbs.

57

Q. How many Elvis impersonators does it take to change a light bulb?

A. Four: one for the money, two for the show, three to get ready and four to go, go, go...

npower | **Book of Light**

Q. How many politicians does it take to screw in a light bulb?
A. I think the question you meant to ask was, "Why hasn't a committee been set up to investigate this?"

58

npower | Book of Light

59

Q. How many supermodels does it take to change a light bulb?
A. None: what do you want me to do – ruin my nails?

60 Q. How many Microsoft software engineers does it take to change a light bulb?
A. None... Bill Gates declares darkness the industry standard!

61 Q. How many atheists does it take to screw in a light bulb?
A. None: atheists never 'see the light'.

62

Q. How many WAGs does it take to change a light bulb?

A. One to change it while the others all comment on her outfit and then try and steal the light!

> Q. How many council workers does it take to change a light bulb?
> A. Four: one doing it and the other three watching!

63

64 Q. How many managers does it take to change a light bulb?
A. It all depends on who they delegate the job to!

65

Q. How many aerobics instructors does it take to change a light bulb?

A. Five: four to do it in perfect synchrony, and one to stand there saying "To the left, and to the left, and to the left, and to the left, and take it out, and put it down, and pick it up, and put it in, and to the right, and to the right, and to the right, and to the right…"

npower — Book of Light

66 **Q. How many dogs does it take to change a light bulb?**
A. Just one Border Collie. It will change the bulb, then redo the wiring as well!

67 **Q. How many Americans does it take to change a light bulb?**
A. 250,000,000: 1 to change it and 249,999,999 to debate whether it was politically correct.

68

Q. How many witches does it take to change a light bulb?

A. Into what?

npower Book of Light

69
Q. How many Vicky Pollards does it take to change a light bulb?
A. Oooh, like, manual labour? Gag me with a spoon! For sure... Like shut up!!!

70
Q. How many accountants does it take to screw in a light bulb?
A. What kind of answer did you have in mind?

71

Q. How many Scrabble players does it take to change a light bulb?

A. I don't actually know, but it's on a triple word score anyway.

npower · Book of Light

72
Q. How many punk rockers does it take to change a light bulb?
A. Two: one to change the bulb and one to eat the old one!

73
Q. How many criminals does it take to change a light bulb?
A. Doesn't matter, they are all a bit shady!

74

Q. How many gardeners does it take to change a light bulb?

A. Three: one to change it, and two to have a debate about whether this is the right time of year to be putting in light bulbs or daffodil bulbs.

npower Book of Light

Q. How many censors does it take to change a light bulb?
A. One to ___ ___ and another to ___ ___ ___ while ___ ___ ___ with a ___.

75

npower — Book of Light

76

Q. How many waitresses does it take to change a light bulb?

A. Three: two to stand around bitching about it and one to go get the manager.

npower — Book of Light

77
Q. How many lumberjacks does it take to change a light bulb?
A. Tree.

78
Q. How many real women does it take to change a light bulb?
A. None: a real woman would have plenty of real men around to do it, and one of them can change the bulb while he's at it.

79

Q. How many Police Officers does it take to change a light bulb?

A. None: it turned itself in.

npower | Book of Light

Q. How many historians does it take to change a light bulb?
A. I dunno, not my period.

80

81

Q. How many safety inspectors does it take to change a light bulb?

A. Four: one to change it, and three to hold the ladder.

npower — Book of Light

82 **Q. How many first year arts students does it take to change a light bulb?**
A. They can't, it's a second year subject.

83 **Q. How many MPs does it take to change a light bulb?**
A. Two: one to buy new wallpaper, and one to explain that it wasn't the light bulb that needed changing, it was the room that needed redecorating!

84

Q. How many boxers does it take to screw in a light bulb?

A. Have you ever tried to change a light bulb with boxing gloves on?

Q. How many Goths does it take to change a light bulb?
A. None: they prefer to cry in the dark.

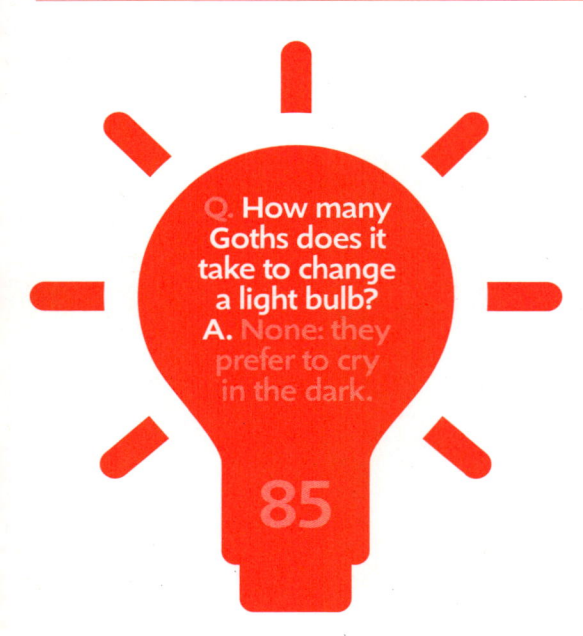

85

86

Q. How many pessimists does it take to screw in a light bulb?
A. None, it's a waste of time because the new bulb probably won't work either.

npower — Book of Light

87

Q. How many sergeant majors does it take to change a light bulb?

A. One two, one two, one two.

npower | Book of Light

88
Q. How many teenage girls does it take to screw in a light bulb?
A. One, but she'll be on the phone for five hours telling all her friends about it.

89
Q. How many Englishmen does it take to screw in a light bulb?
A. What do you mean change it? It's a perfectly good bloody bulb! We have had it for a thousand years and it has worked just fine.

90

Q. How many surgeons does it take to replace a light bulb?

A. Three: we'd also like to remove the socket, as you aren't using it now.

Q. How many camels does it take to change a light bulb?
A. Two: one on standby in case the other gets the hump.

91

npower — Book of Light

92

Q. How many chickens does it take to change a light bulb?

A. None: they're all far too busy crossing the road.

npower | Book of Light

93

Q. How many pantomime dames does it take to change a light bulb?
A. One.
"Oh no it doesn't!"
"Oh yes it does!"
"Oh no it doesn't!"
"Oh yes it does!"

94

Q. How many university graduates does it take to change a light bulb?

A. One, but may take up to seven years!

npower | **Book of Light**

Q. How many chiropractors does it take to change a light bulb?
A. Only one, but it takes nine visits.

95

npower   Book of Light

96

Q. How many psychoanalysts does it take to change a light bulb?
A. It's not really a case of how many psychoanalysts, more that the light bulb has got to want to change.

97

**Q. How many Zen masters does it take to screw in a light bulb?
A. None: Zen masters carry their own light.**

npower — Book of Light

100

Q. How many aerospace engineers does it take to change a light bulb?

A. None: it's not rocket science.

npower, official energy partner to Red Nose Day 2007,
is celebrating the iconic light bulb joke, as a way of raising
awareness to energy saving in a light-hearted manner,
while raising money for Comic Relief at the same time.

www.npower.com
www.rednoseday.com

npower — Book of Light

98

Q. How many penguins does it take to change a light bulb?

A. One, and then two thousand to huddle around it rubbing their flippers together.

99

**Q. How many American wrestlers does it take to change a light bulb?
A. Three:** one to yank the old bulb out, throw it to the floor, try and jump on it from a great height and act real surprised when it rolls out of the way at the last minute; one to pretend to twist the new one round so far it nearly breaks and some guy in a black-and-white stripy uniform (whose function is never made quite clear) to protest about something or other, to the complete indifference of the bulb changers.